GRAPHIC LIBRARY ™

GRAPHIC BIOGRAPHIES

SACAGAWEA
❧ JOURNEY INTO THE WEST ❧

by Jessica Gunderson
illustrated by Cynthia Martin
and Barbara Schulz

Consultant:
Troy Rollen Johnson, PhD
American Indian Studies
California State University, Long Beach

Capstone press®
Mankato, Minnesota

Graphic Library is published by Capstone Press,
1710 Roe Crest Drive, North Mankato, Minnesota 56003.
www.capstonepub.com

Printed in the United States of America in Stevens Point, Wisconsin.
022014
008025R

Library of Congress Cataloging-in-Publication Data
Gunderson, Jessica Sarah, 1976–
Sacagawea : journey into the west / by Jessica Gunderson ; illustrated by Cynthia Martin and Barbara Schulz.
p. cm. — (Graphic library. Graphic biographies)
Includes bibliographical references and index.
ISBN-13: 978-0-7368-6499-2 (hardcover)
ISBN-10: 0-7368-6499-7 (hardcover)
ISBN-13: 978-0-7368-9663-4 (softcover pbk.)
ISBN-10: 0-7368-9663-5 (softcover pbk.)
1. Sacagawea—Juvenile literature. 2. Shoshoni women—Biography—Juvenile literature. 3. Shoshoni Indians—Biography—Juvenile literature. 4. Lewis and Clark Expedition (1804–1806)—Juvenile literature. I. Martin, Cynthia, 1961– , ill. II. Schulz, Barbara, 1948– , ill. III. Title. IV. Series.
F592.7.S123G86 2007
970.004'97—dc22 2006007308

Summary: In graphic novel format, tells the story of Sacagawea, the teenage Shoshone mother who traveled with the Lewis and Clark expedition as an interpreter.

Designer
Alison Thiele

Editor
Gillia Olson

Editor's note: Direct quotations from primary sources are indicated by a yellow background.

Direct quotations appear on the following pages:
Page 17, from October 13, 1805, journal entry by William Clark; Page 18, from November 24, 1805, journal entry by William Clark; Page 19, from January 6, 1806, journal entry by William Clark; as reprinted in *The Lewis and Clark Journals: An American Epic of Discovery: The Abridgement of the Definitive Nebraska Edition*, edited by Gary E. Moulton (Lincoln, Neb.: University of Nebraska Press, 2003.)
Page 24, from William Clark's letter to Toussaint Charbonneau, dated August 20, 1806, reprinted in *Sacajawea: A Guide and Interpreter of the Lewis and Clark Expedition, with an Account of the Travels of Toussaint Charbonneau and of Jean Baptiste, the Expedition Papoose*, by Grace Raymond Hebard (Glendale, Cal.: Arthur H. Clark Company, 1957).

TABLE OF CONTENTS

CHAPTER 1
CAPTURE!

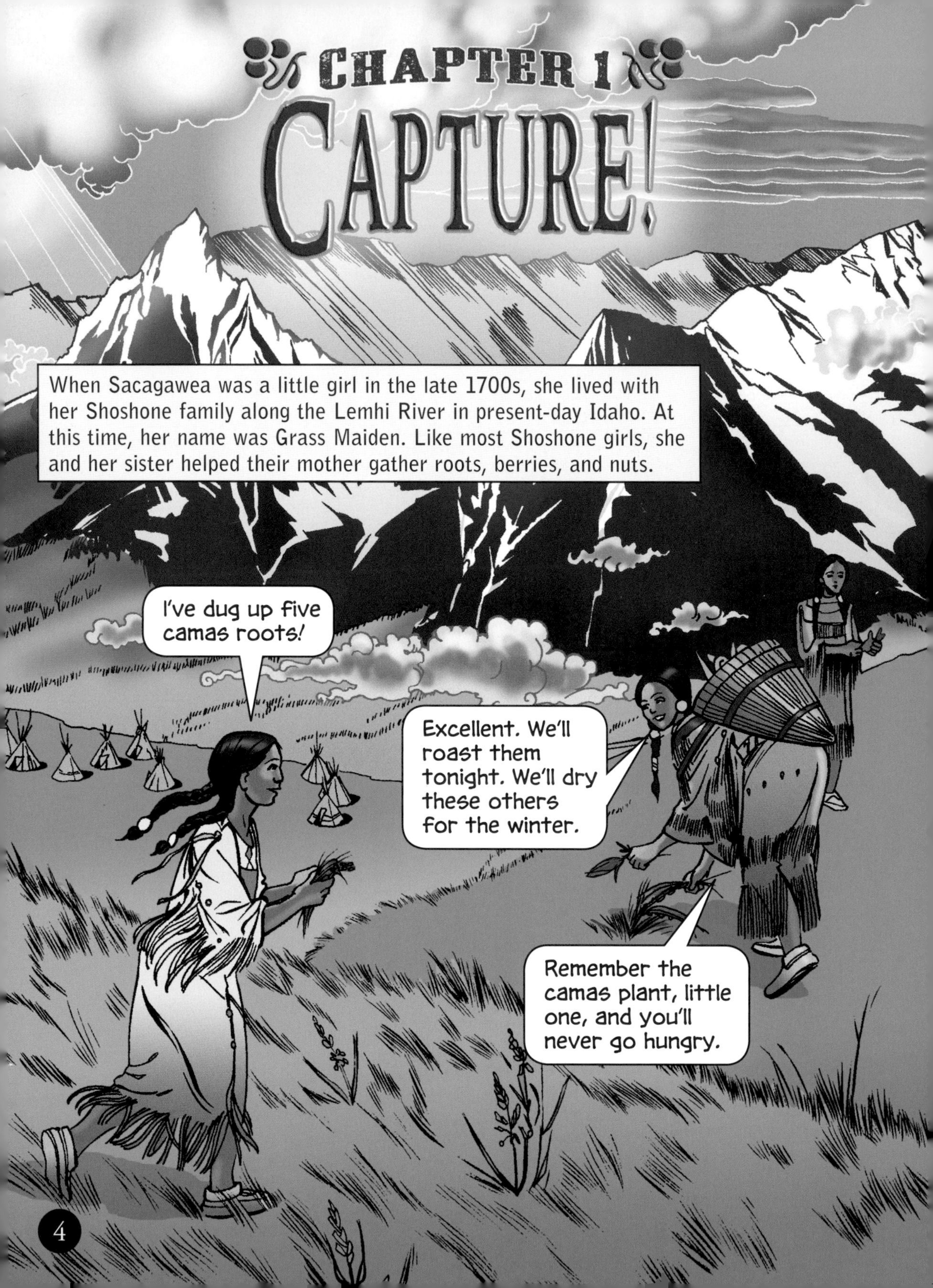
When Sacagawea was a little girl in the late 1700s, she lived with her Shoshone family along the Lemhi River in present-day Idaho. At this time, her name was Grass Maiden. Like most Shoshone girls, she and her sister helped their mother gather roots, berries, and nuts.
I've dug up five camas roots!
Excellent. We'll roast them tonight. We'll dry these others for the winter.
Remember the camas plant, little one, and you'll never go hungry.

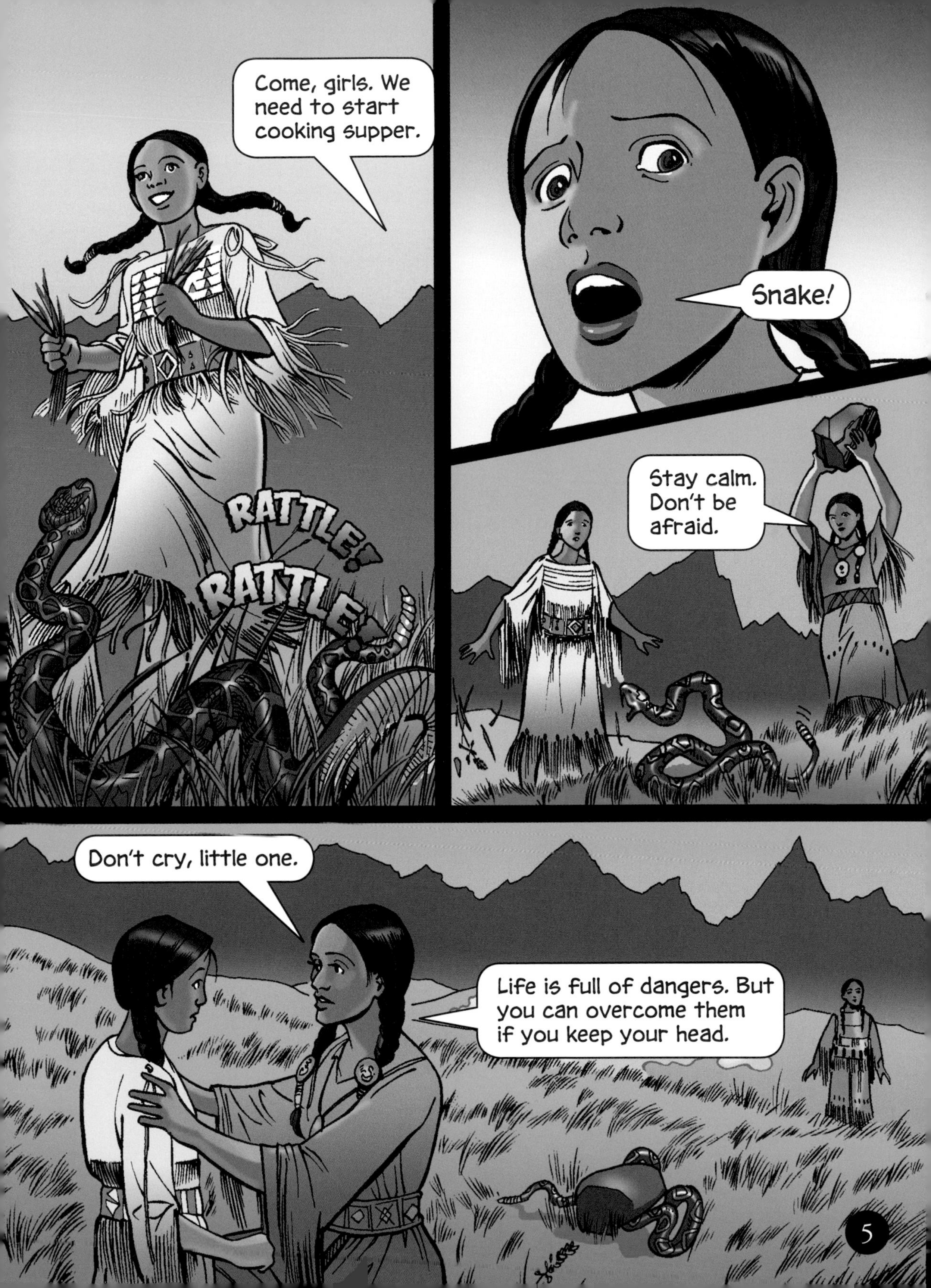
Come, girls. We need to start cooking supper.
RATTLE! RATTLE!
Snake!
Stay calm. Don't be afraid.
Don't cry, little one.
Life is full of dangers. But you can overcome them if you keep your head.

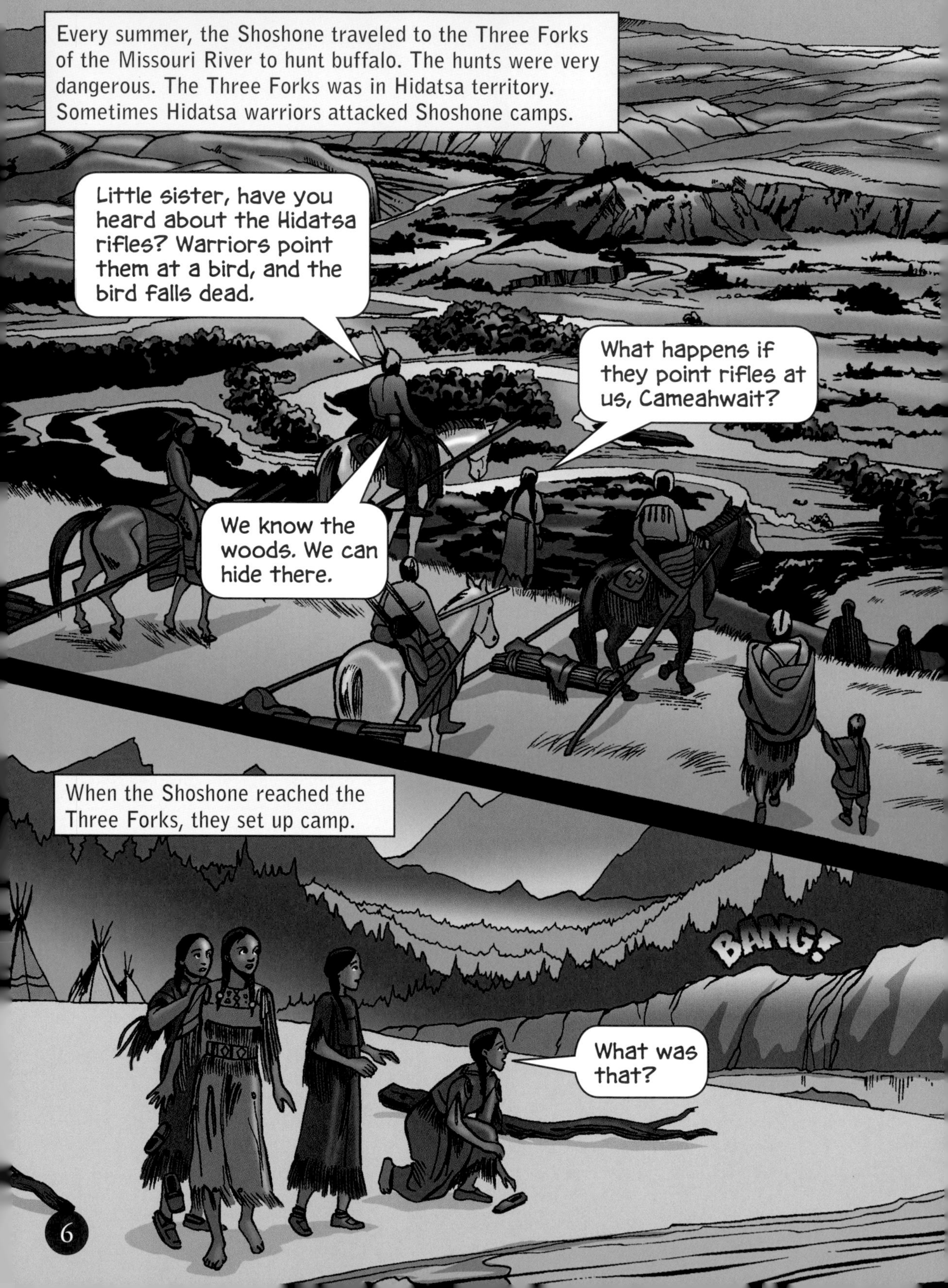
Every summer, the Shoshone traveled to the Three Forks of the Missouri River to hunt buffalo. The hunts were very dangerous. The Three Forks was in Hidatsa territory. Sometimes Hidatsa warriors attacked Shoshone camps.
Little sister, have you heard about the Hidatsa rifles? Warriors point them at a bird, and the bird falls dead.
What happens if they point rifles at us, Cameahwait?
We know the woods. We can hide there.
When the Shoshone reached the Three Forks, they set up camp.
BANG!
What was that?

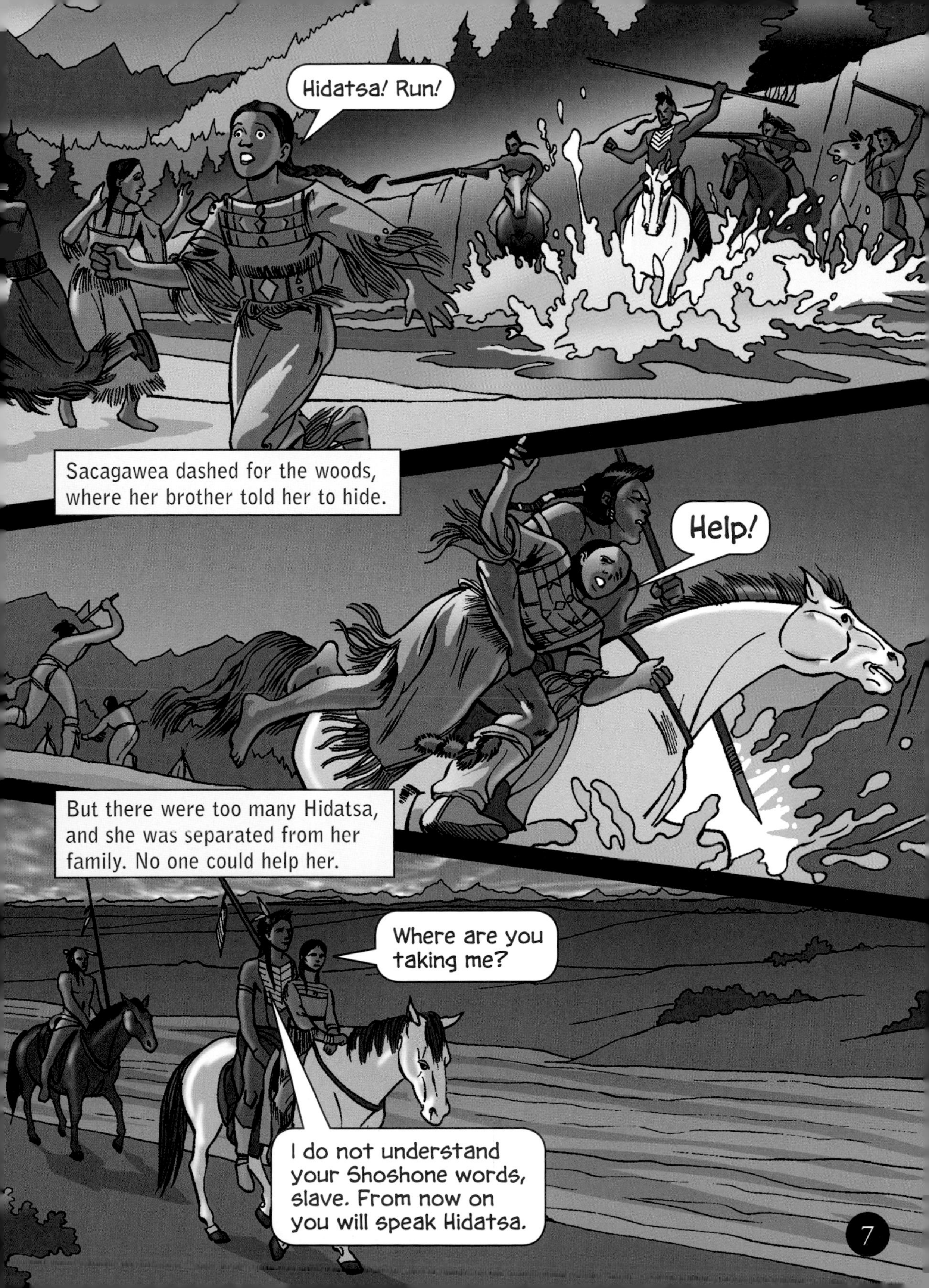

Hidatsa! Run!
Sacagawea dashed for the woods, where her brother told her to hide.
Help!
But there were too many Hidatsa, and she was separated from her family. No one could help her.
Where are you taking me?
I do not understand your Shoshone words, slave. From now on you will speak Hidatsa.

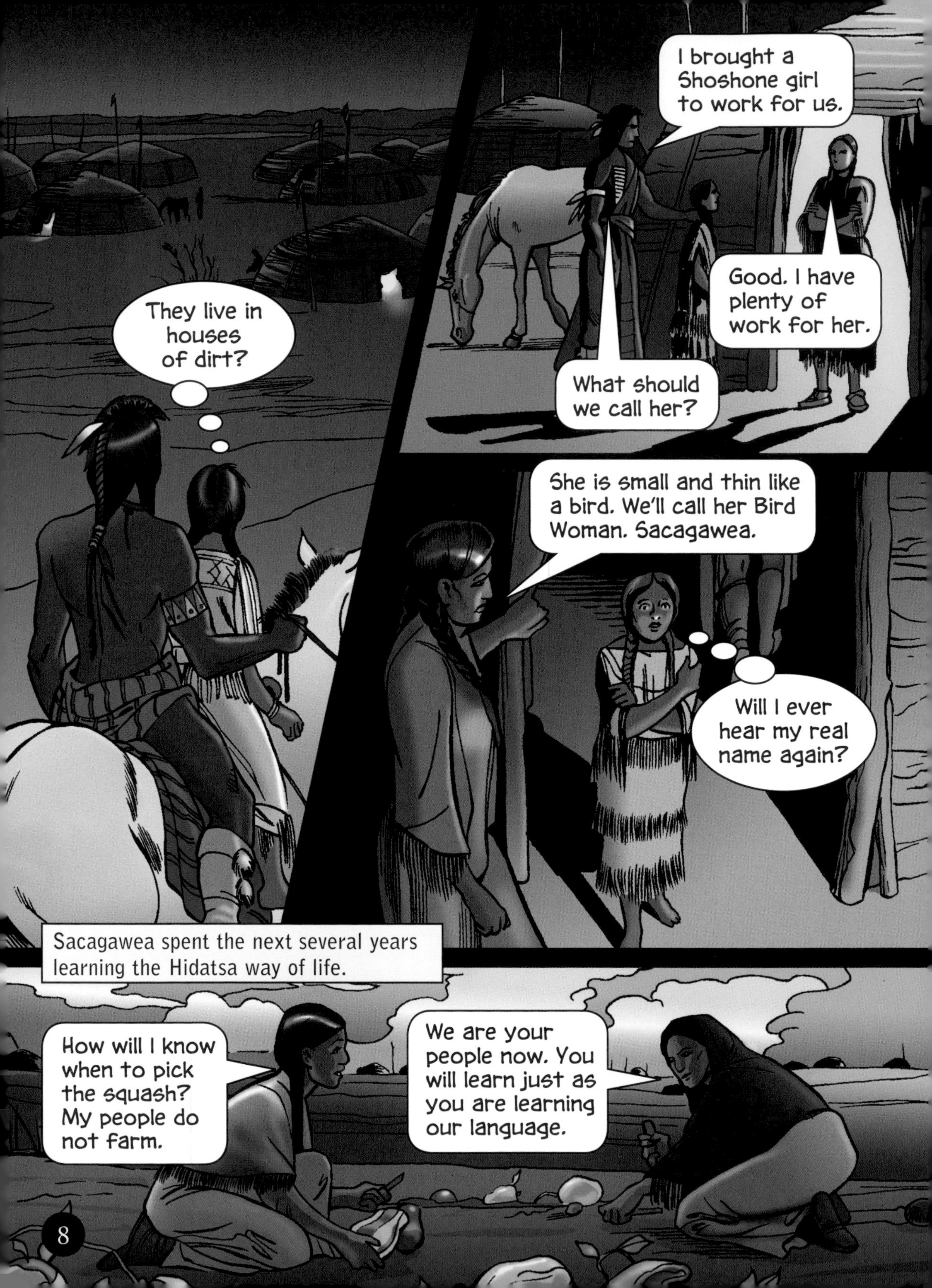
They live in houses of dirt?
I brought a Shoshone girl to work for us.
What should we call her?
Good. I have plenty of work for her.
She is small and thin like a bird. We'll call her Bird Woman. Sacagawea.
Will I ever hear my real name again?
Sacagawea spent the next several years learning the Hidatsa way of life.
How will I know when to pick the squash? My people do not farm.
We are your people now. You will learn just as you are learning our language.

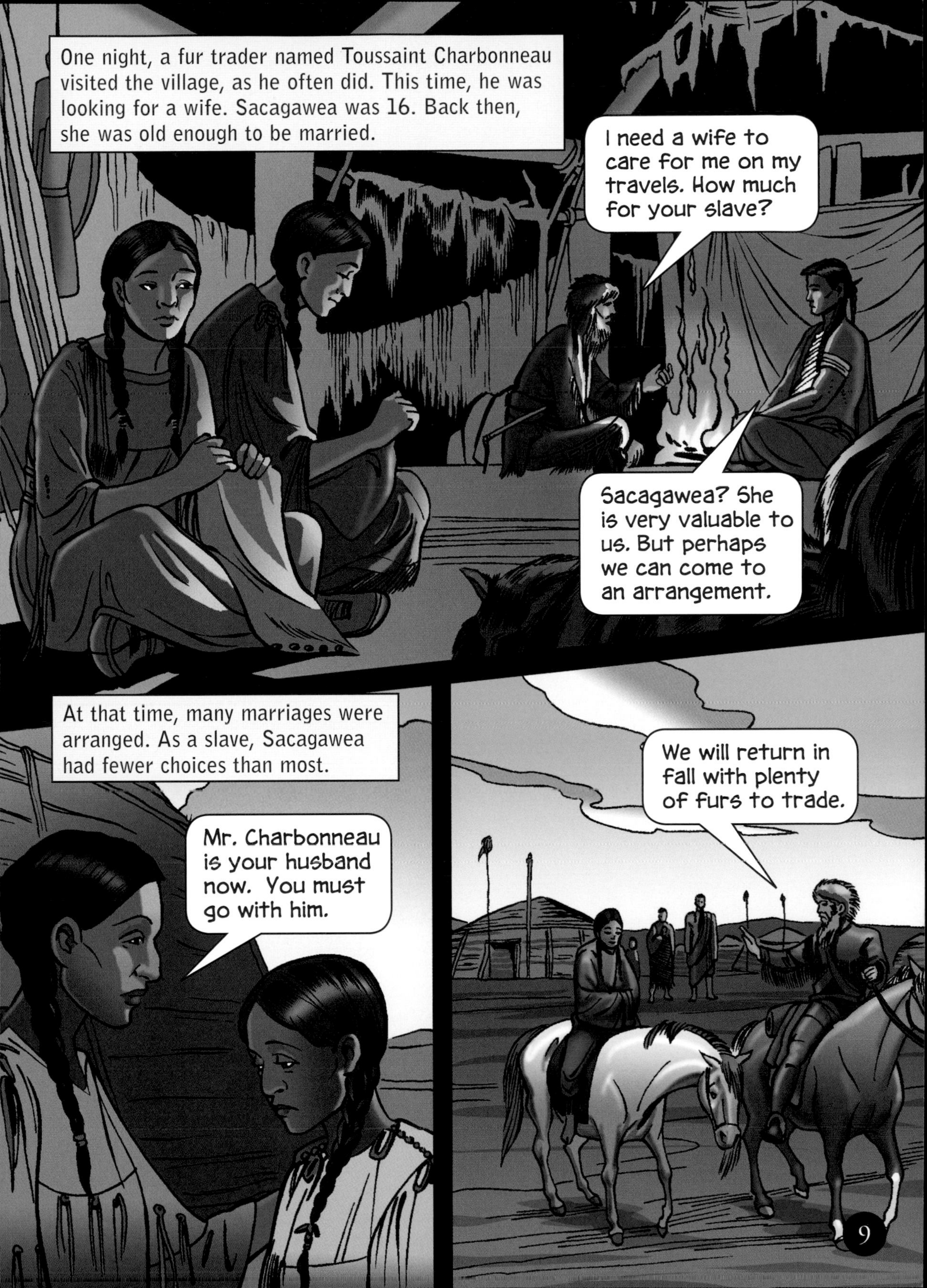

One night, a fur trader named Toussaint Charbonneau visited the village, as he often did. This time, he was looking for a wife. Sacagawea was 16. Back then, she was old enough to be married.
I need a wife to care for me on my travels. How much for your slave?
Sacagawea? She is very valuable to us. But perhaps we can come to an arrangement.
At that time, many marriages were arranged. As a slave, Sacagawea had fewer choices than most.
Mr. Charbonneau is your husband now. You must go with him.
We will return in fall with plenty of furs to trade.

CHAPTER 2
THE JOURNEY WESTWARD

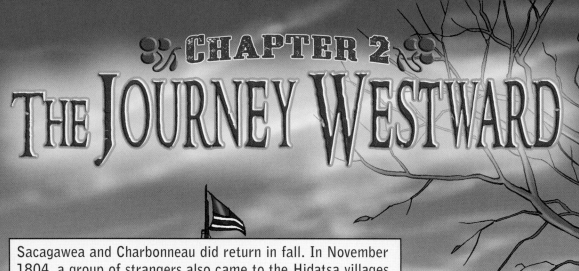

Sacagawea and Charbonneau did return in fall. In November 1804, a group of strangers also came to the Hidatsa villages. Led by Meriwether Lewis and William Clark, these men were on an exploring mission for the United States.

It's the men I've heard other fur traders talking about. They are from the cities far east of here. They're trying to find a water route all the way west, to the Pacific Ocean.

Why?

Ships could then bring trade goods all the way to the ocean and beyond to other lands.

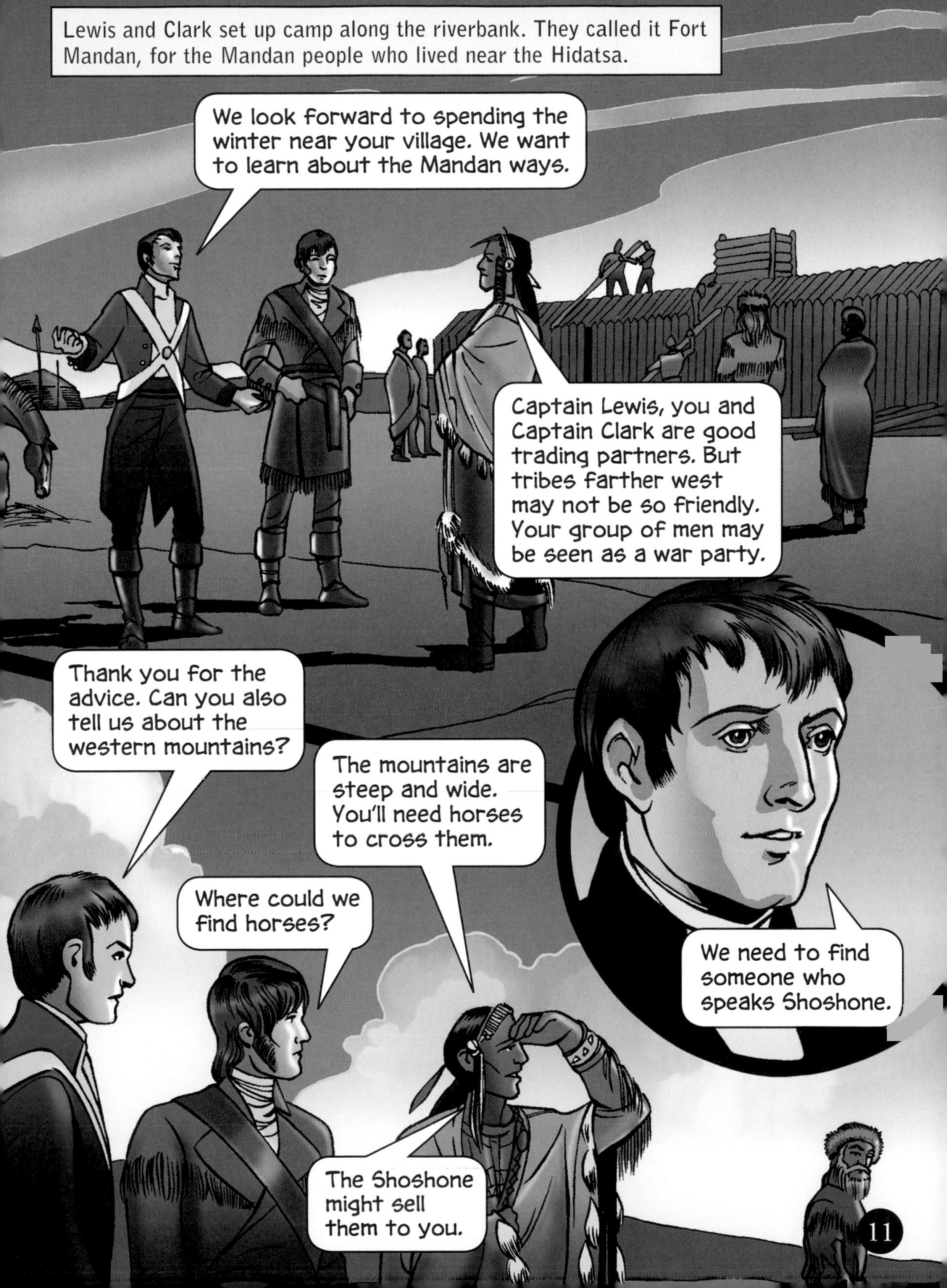
Lewis and Clark set up camp along the riverbank. They called it Fort Mandan, for the Mandan people who lived near the Hidatsa.
We look forward to spending the winter near your village. We want to learn about the Mandan ways.
Captain Lewis, you and Captain Clark are good trading partners. But tribes farther west may not be so friendly. Your group of men may be seen as a war party.
Thank you for the advice. Can you also tell us about the western mountains?
The mountains are steep and wide. You'll need horses to cross them.
We need to find someone who speaks Shoshone.
Where could we find horses?
The Shoshone might sell them to you.

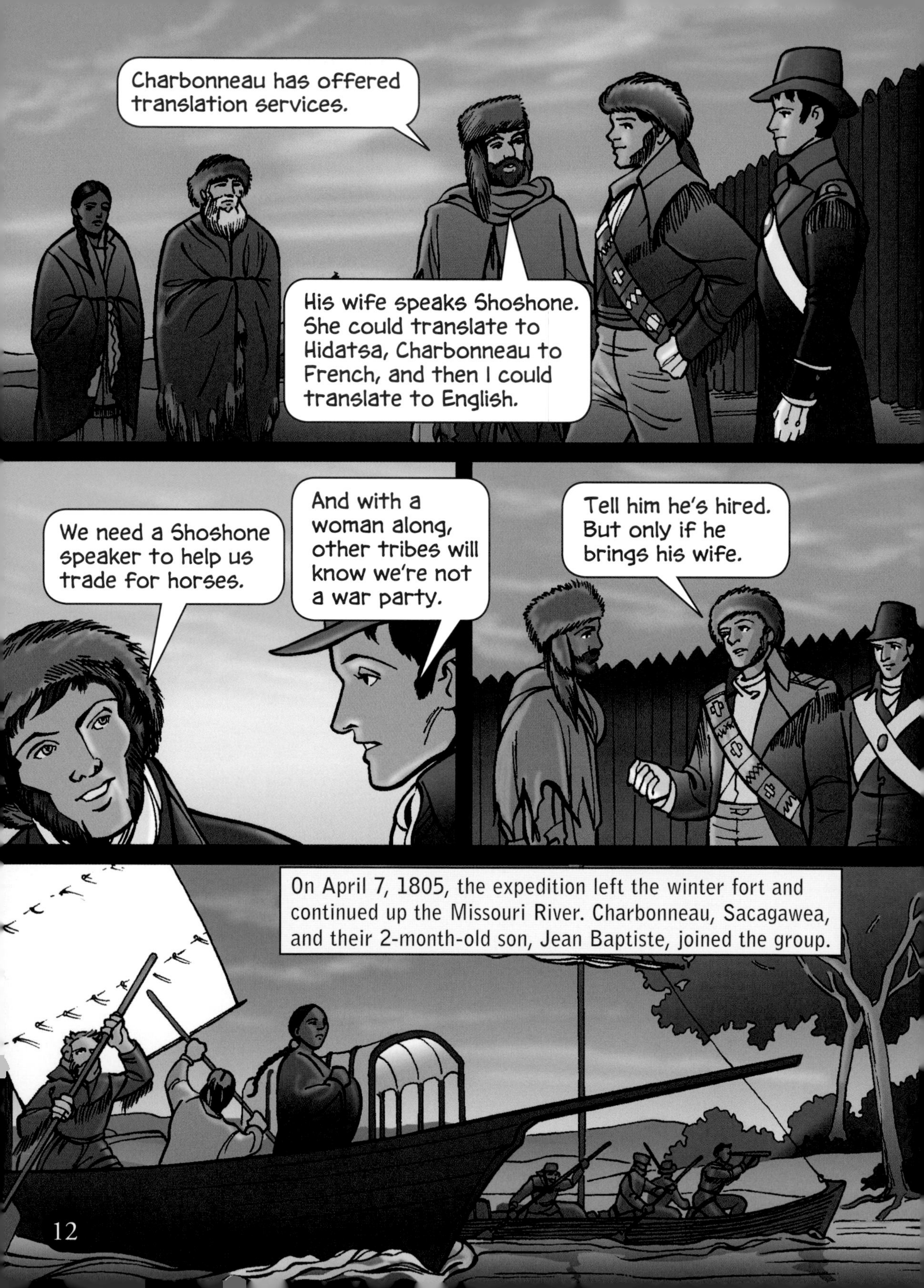
Charbonneau has offered translation services.
His wife speaks Shoshone. She could translate to Hidatsa, Charbonneau to French, and then I could translate to English.
We need a Shoshone speaker to help us trade for horses.
And with a woman along, other tribes will know we're not a war party.
Tell him he's hired. But only if he brings his wife.
On April 7, 1805, the expedition left the winter fort and continued up the Missouri River. Charbonneau, Sacagawea, and their 2-month-old son, Jean Baptiste, joined the group.

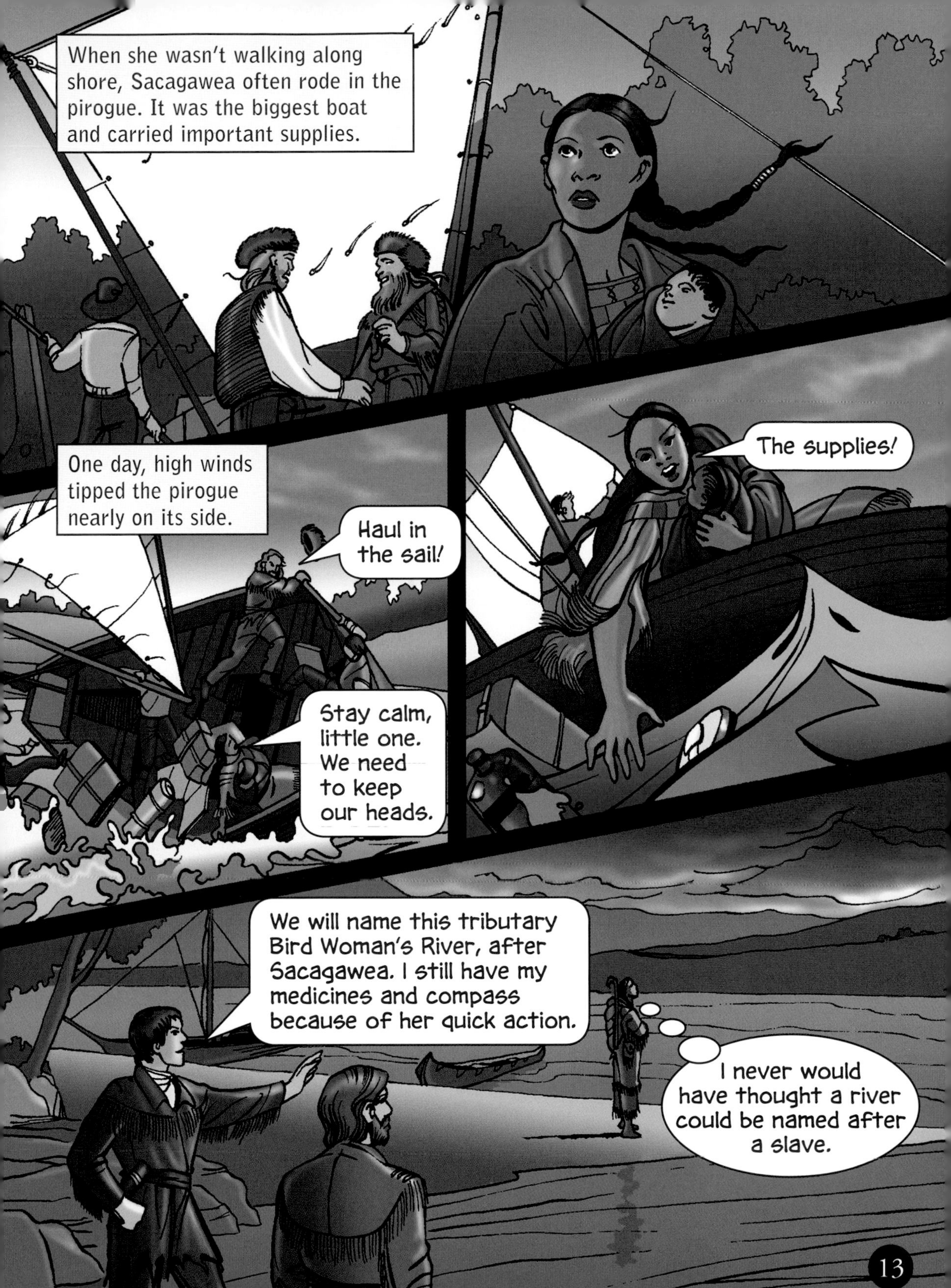

When she wasn't walking along shore, Sacagawea often rode in the pirogue. It was the biggest boat and carried important supplies.
One day, high winds tipped the pirogue nearly on its side.
Haul in the sail!
Stay calm, little one. We need to keep our heads.
The supplies!
We will name this tributary Bird Woman's River, after Sacagawea. I still have my medicines and compass because of her quick action.
I never would have thought a river could be named after a slave.

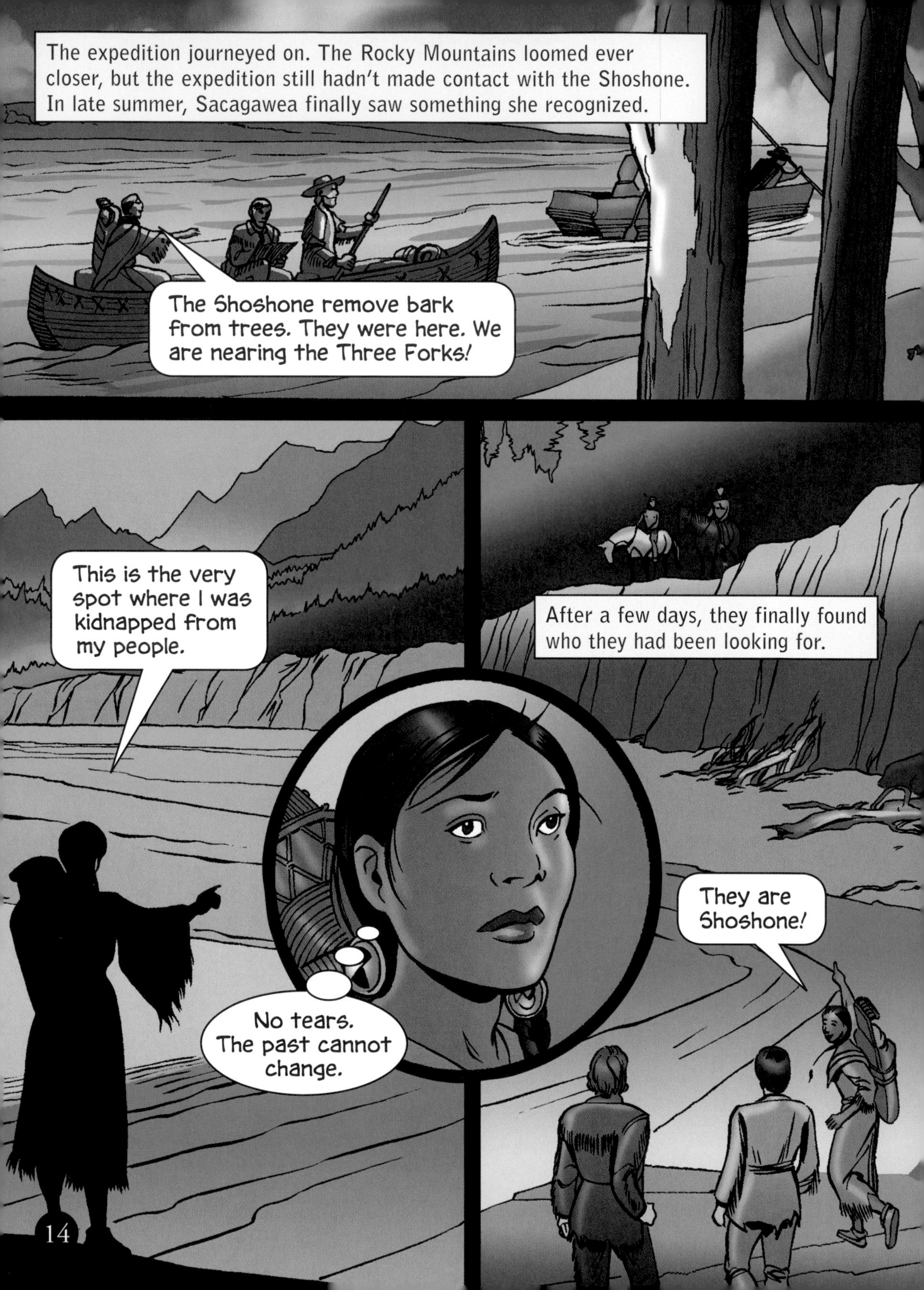
The expedition journeyed on. The Rocky Mountains loomed ever closer, but the expedition still hadn't made contact with the Shoshone. In late summer, Sacagawea finally saw something she recognized.
The Shoshone remove bark from trees. They were here. We are nearing the Three Forks!
This is the very spot where I was kidnapped from my people.
No tears. The past cannot change.
After a few days, they finally found who they had been looking for.
They are Shoshone!

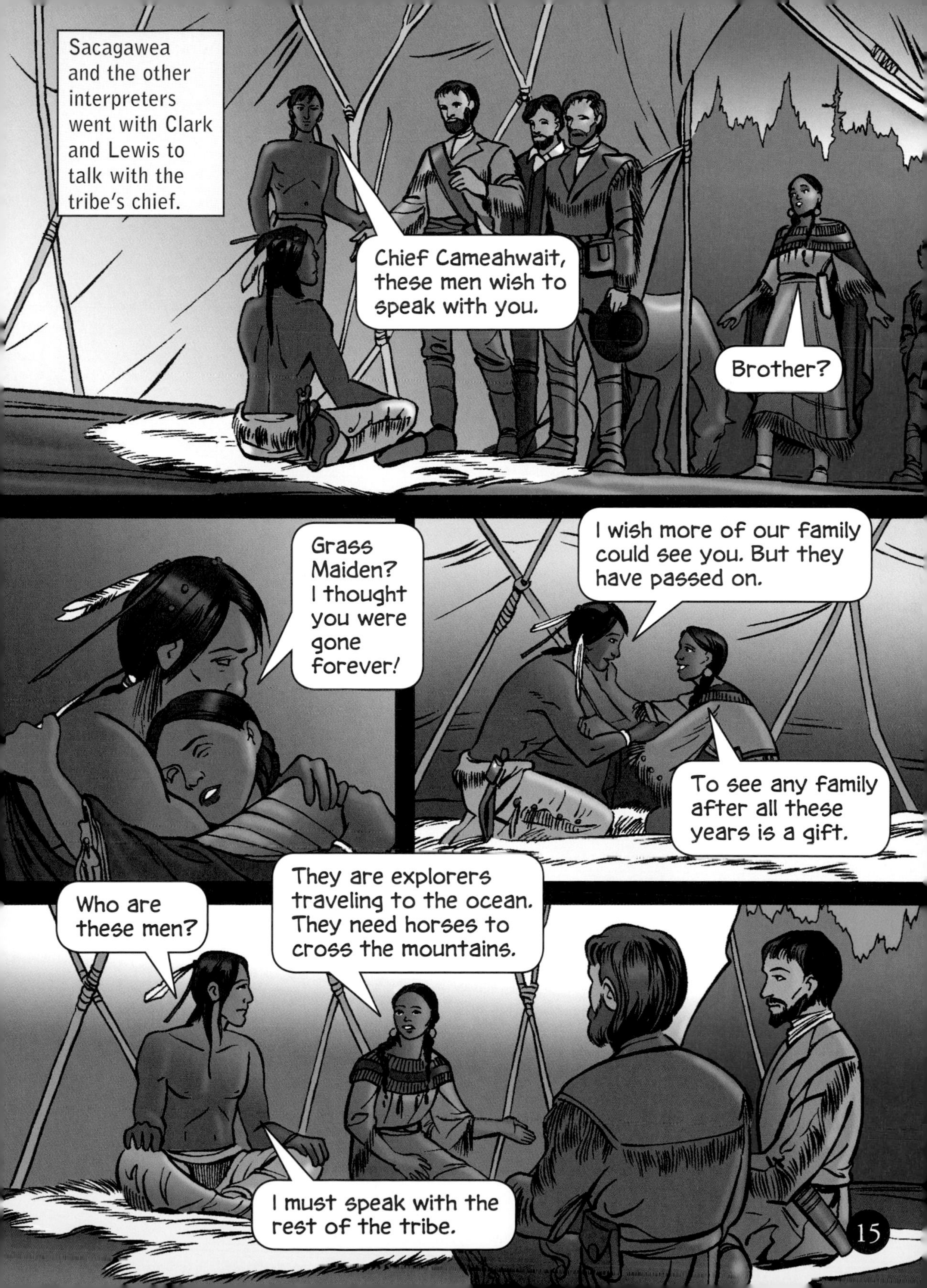
Sacagawea and the other interpreters went with Clark and Lewis to talk with the tribe's chief.
Chief Cameahwait, these men wish to speak with you.
Brother?
Grass Maiden? I thought you were gone forever!
I wish more of our family could see you. But they have passed on.
To see any family after all these years is a gift.
Who are these men?
They are explorers traveling to the ocean. They need horses to cross the mountains.
I must speak with the rest of the tribe.

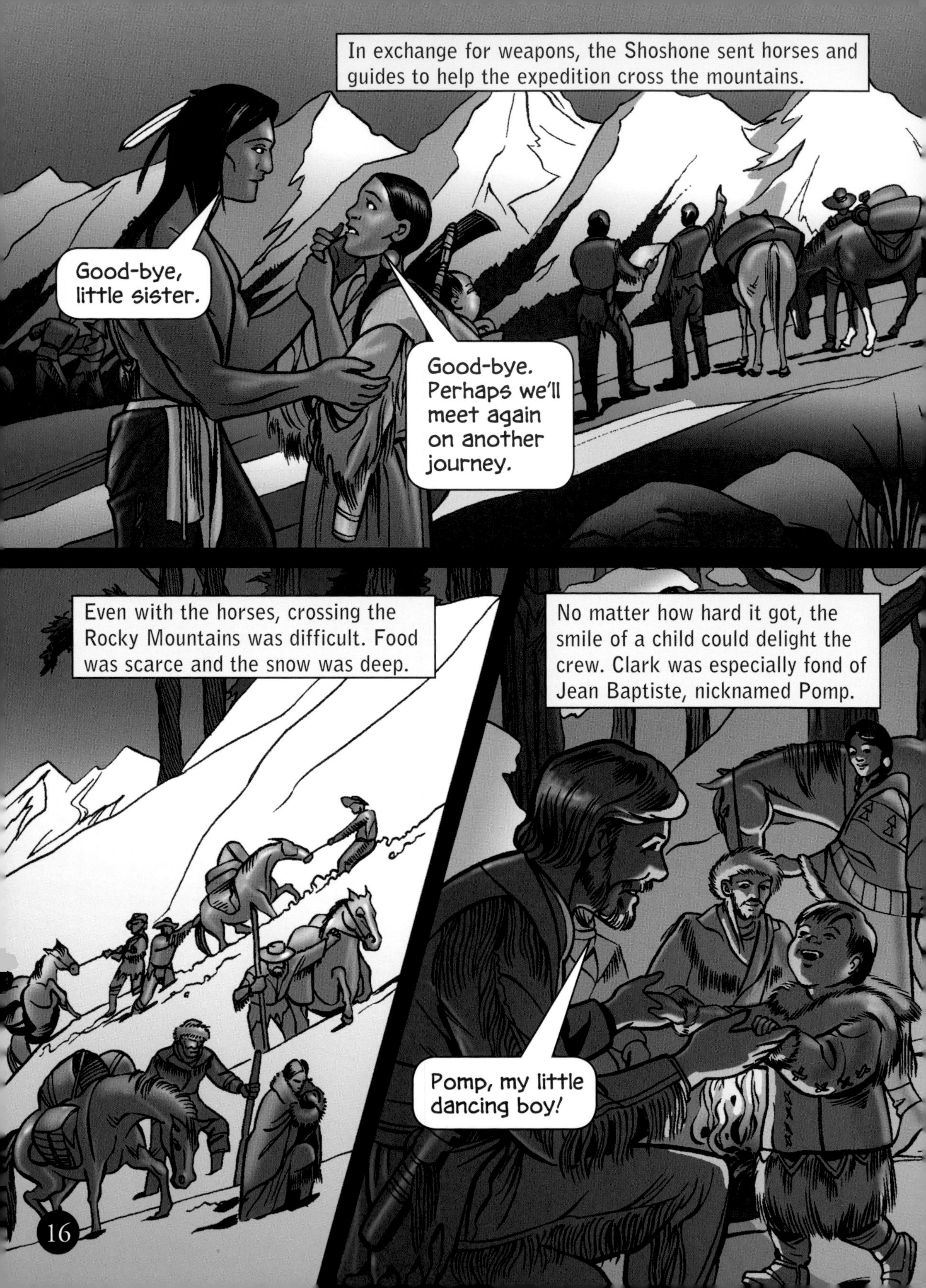
In exchange for weapons, the Shoshone sent horses and guides to help the expedition cross the mountains.
Good-bye, little sister.
Good-bye. Perhaps we'll meet again on another journey.
Even with the horses, crossing the Rocky Mountains was difficult. Food was scarce and the snow was deep.
No matter how hard it got, the smile of a child could delight the crew. Clark was especially fond of Jean Baptiste, nicknamed Pomp.
Pomp, my little dancing boy!

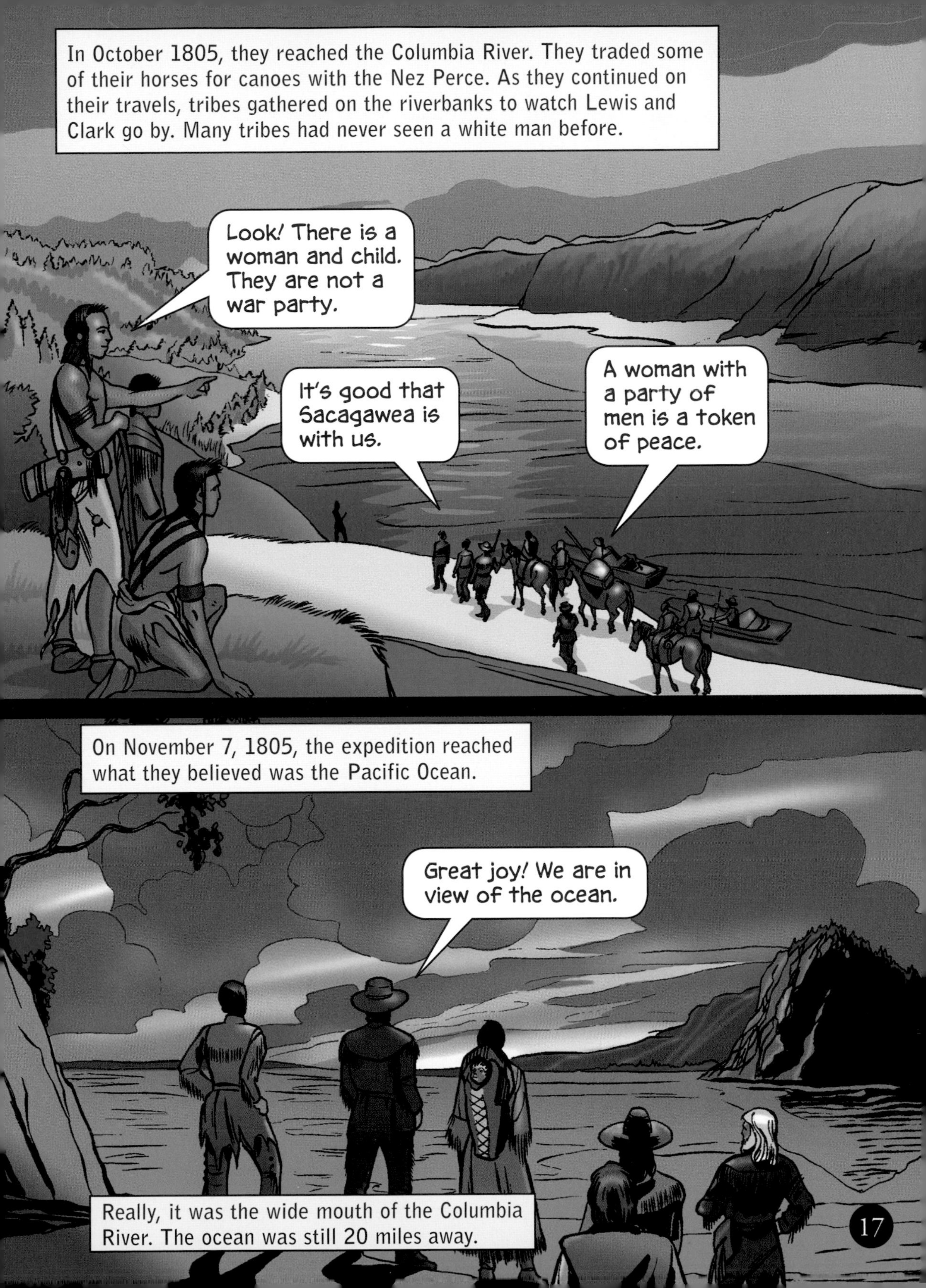
In October 1805, they reached the Columbia River. They traded some of their horses for canoes with the Nez Perce. As they continued on their travels, tribes gathered on the riverbanks to watch Lewis and Clark go by. Many tribes had never seen a white man before.
Look! There is a woman and child. They are not a war party.
It's good that Sacagawea is with us.
A woman with a party of men is a token of peace.
On November 7, 1805, the expedition reached what they believed was the Pacific Ocean.
Great joy! We are in view of the ocean.
Really, it was the wide mouth of the Columbia River. The ocean was still 20 miles away.

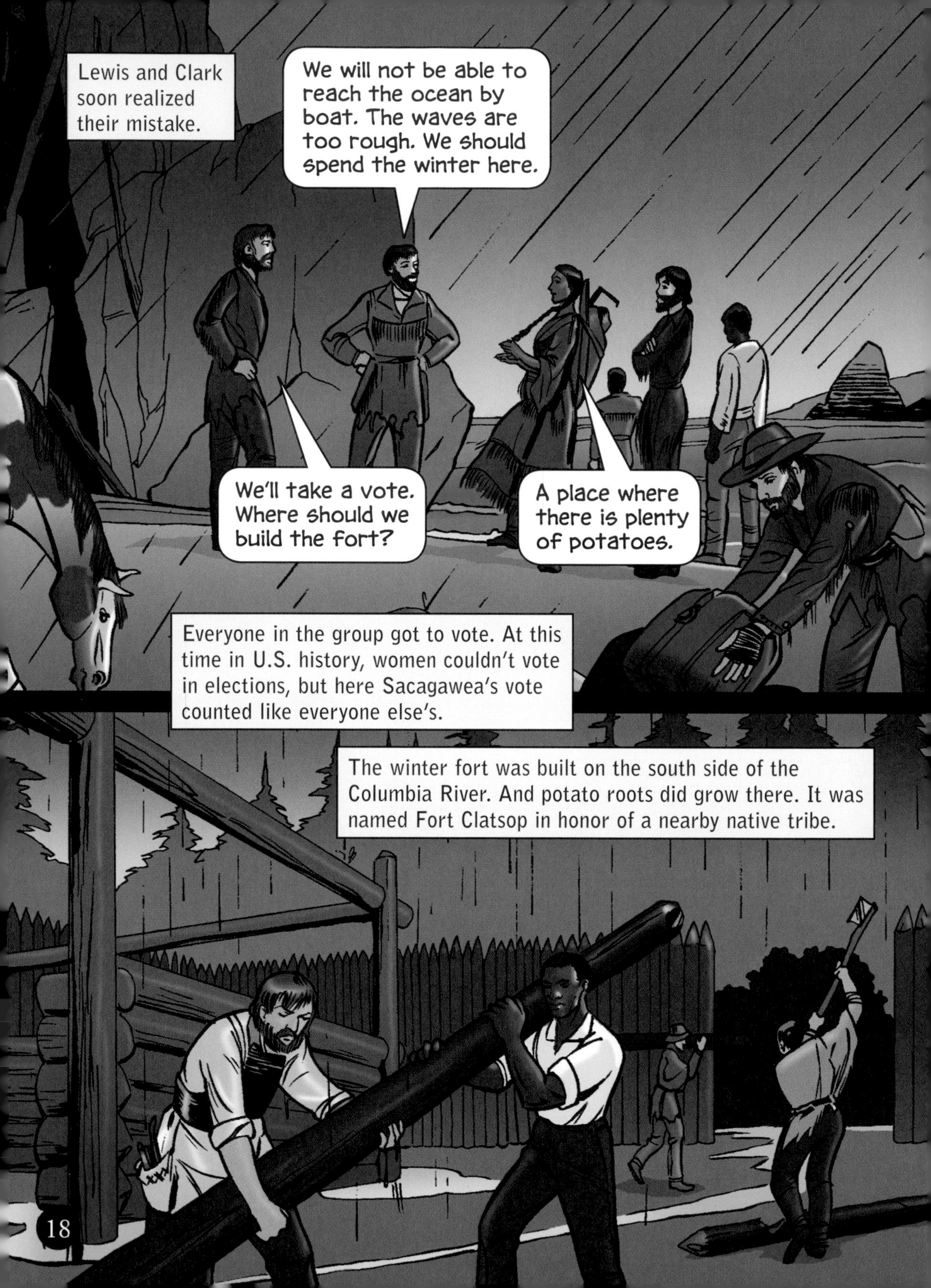

Lewis and Clark soon realized their mistake.
We will not be able to reach the ocean by boat. The waves are too rough. We should spend the winter here.
We'll take a vote. Where should we build the fort?
A place where there is plenty of potatoes.
Everyone in the group got to vote. At this time in U.S. history, women couldn't vote in elections, but here Sacagawea's vote counted like everyone else's.
The winter fort was built on the south side of the Columbia River. And potato roots did grow there. It was named Fort Clatsop in honor of a nearby native tribe.

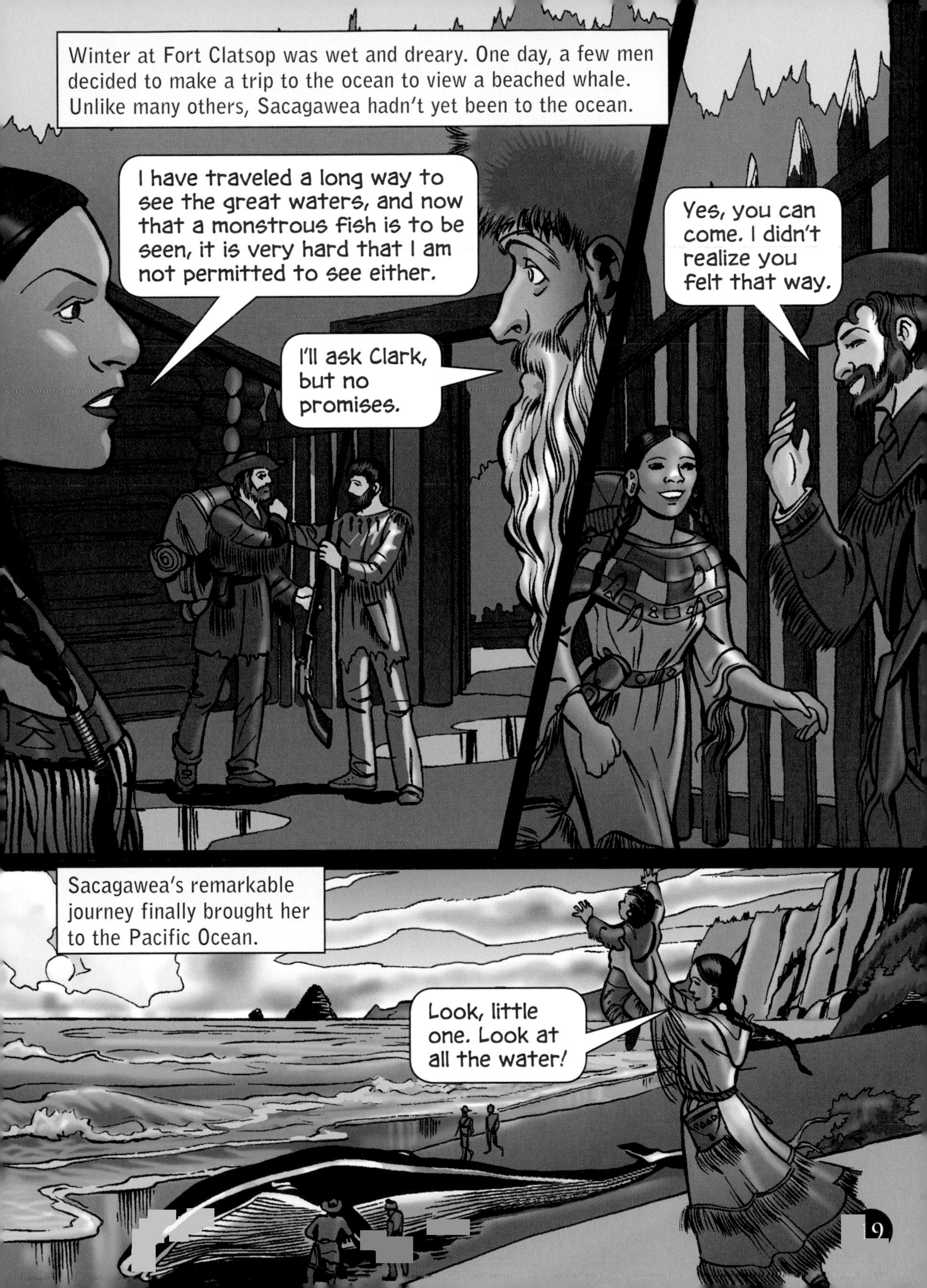
Winter at Fort Clatsop was wet and dreary. One day, a few men decided to make a trip to the ocean to view a beached whale. Unlike many others, Sacagawea hadn't yet been to the ocean.
I have traveled a long way to see the great waters, and now that a monstrous fish is to be seen, it is very hard that I am not permitted to see either.
I'll ask Clark, but no promises.
Yes, you can come. I didn't realize you felt that way.
Sacagawea's remarkable journey finally brought her to the Pacific Ocean.
Look, little one. Look at all the water!

CHAPTER 3
THE RETURN TRIP

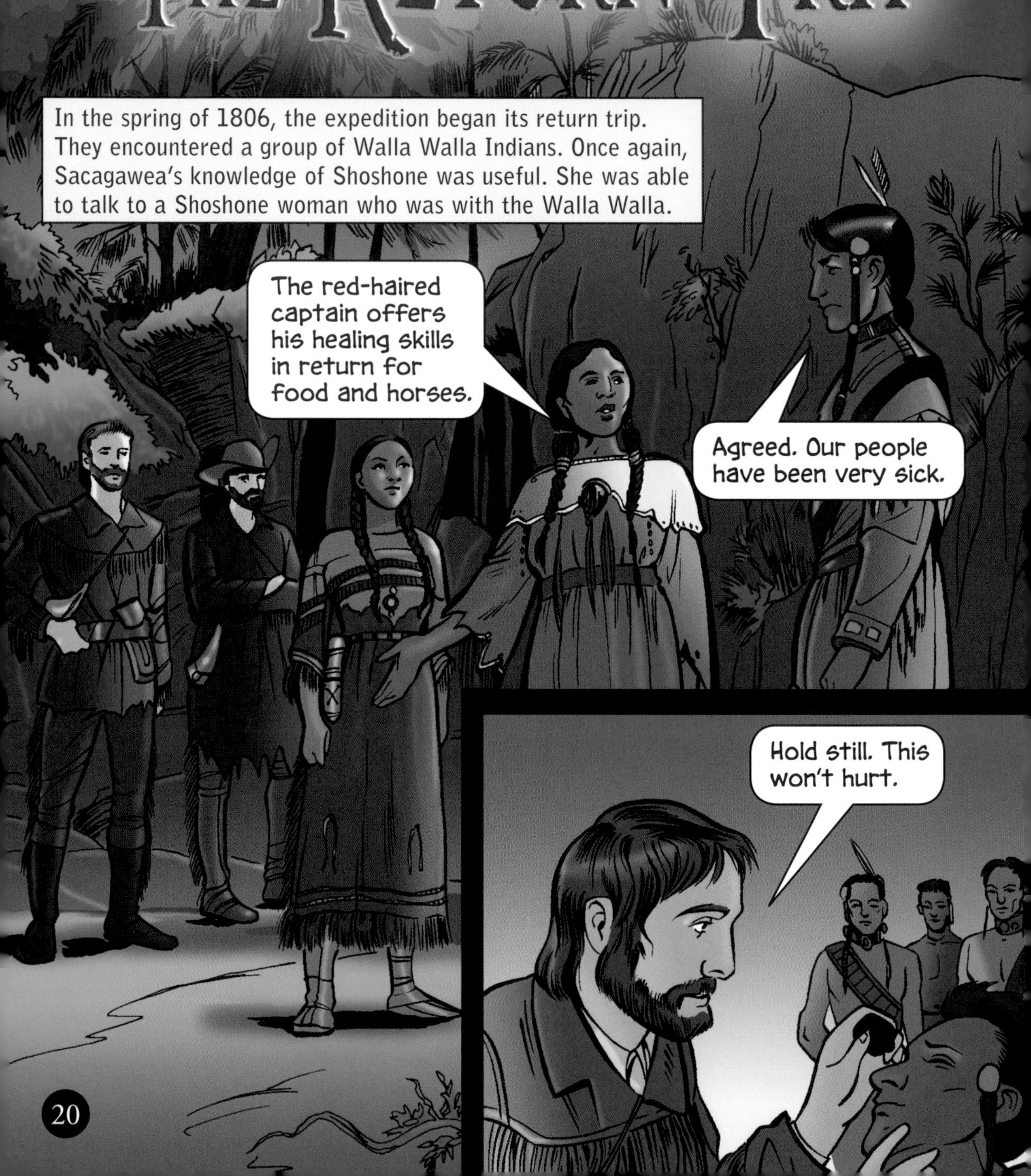
In the spring of 1806, the expedition began its return trip. They encountered a group of Walla Walla Indians. Once again, Sacagawea's knowledge of Shoshone was useful. She was able to talk to a Shoshone woman who was with the Walla Walla.
The red-haired captain offers his healing skills in return for food and horses.
Agreed. Our people have been very sick.
Hold still. This won't hurt.

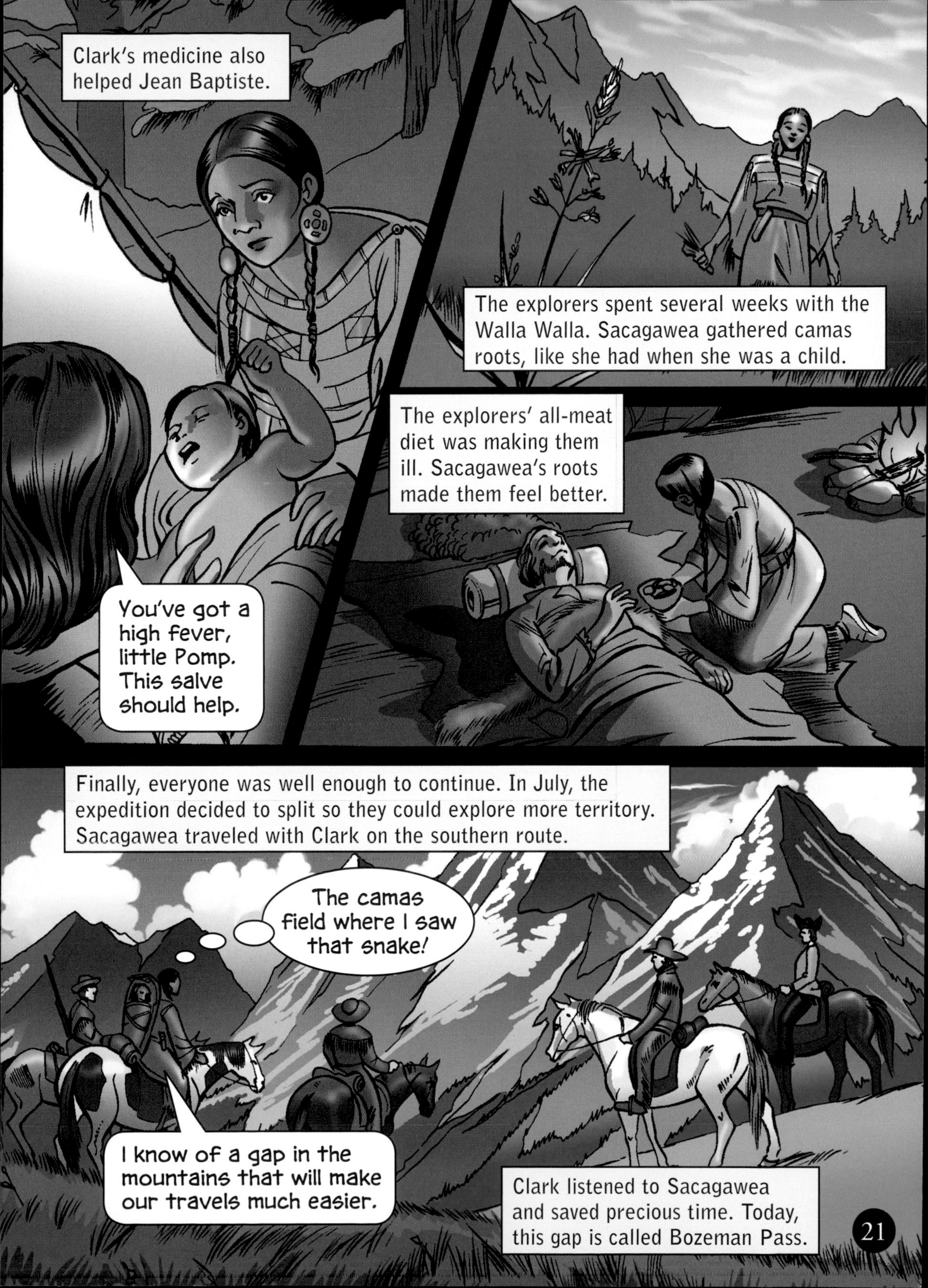

Clark's medicine also helped Jean Baptiste.
You've got a high fever, little Pomp. This salve should help.
The explorers spent several weeks with the Walla Walla. Sacagawea gathered camas roots, like she had when she was a child.
The explorers' all-meat diet was making them ill. Sacagawea's roots made them feel better.
Finally, everyone was well enough to continue. In July, the expedition decided to split so they could explore more territory. Sacagawea traveled with Clark on the southern route.
The camas field where I saw that snake!
I know of a gap in the mountains that will make our travels much easier.
Clark listened to Sacagawea and saved precious time. Today, this gap is called Bozeman Pass.

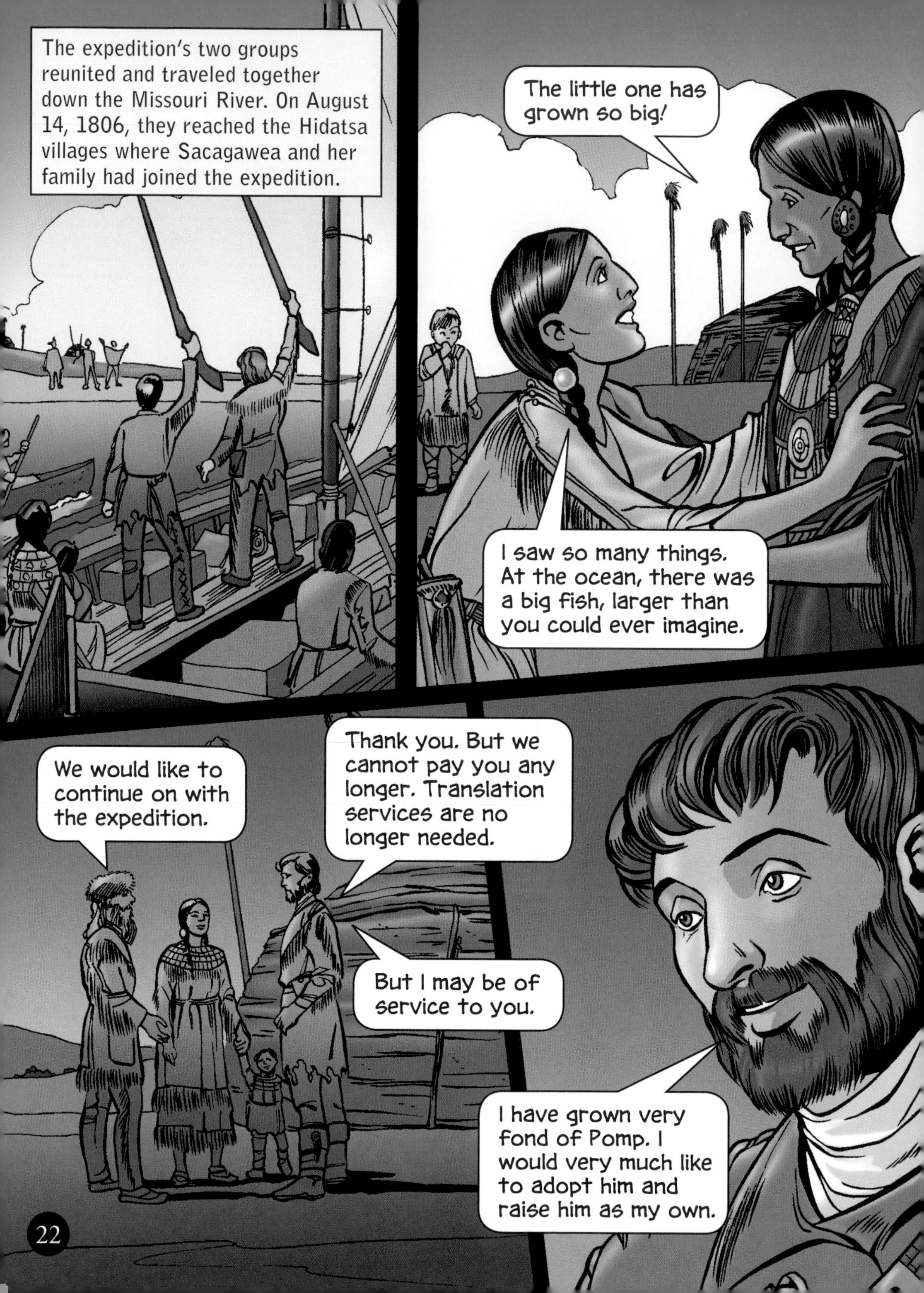
The expedition's two groups reunited and traveled together down the Missouri River. On August 14, 1806, they reached the Hidatsa villages where Sacagawea and her family had joined the expedition.
The little one has grown so big!
I saw so many things. At the ocean, there was a big fish, larger than you could ever imagine.
We would like to continue on with the expedition.
Thank you. But we cannot pay you any longer. Translation services are no longer needed.
But I may be of service to you.
I have grown very fond of Pomp. I would very much like to adopt him and raise him as my own.

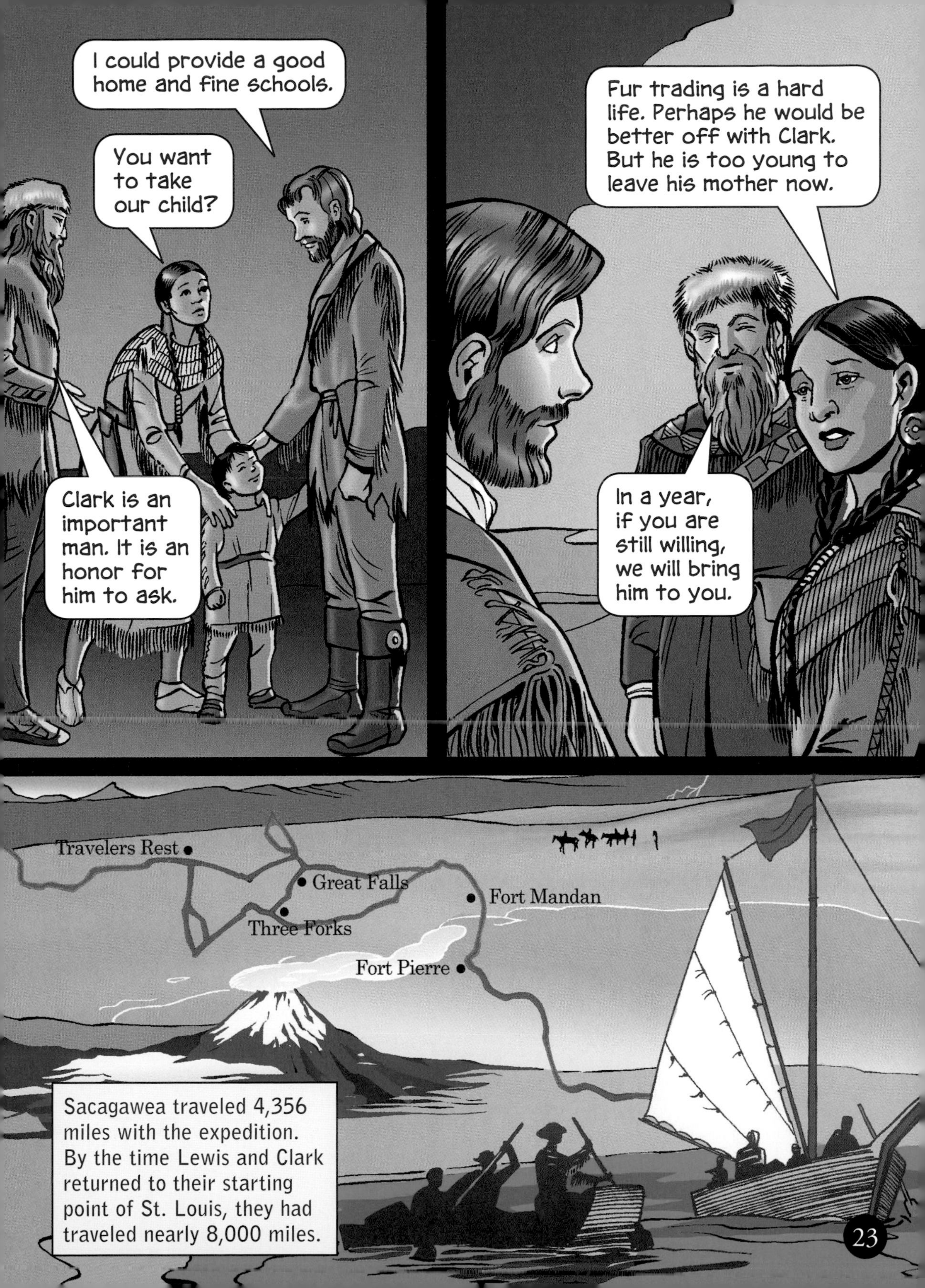

I could provide a good home and fine schools.
You want to take our child?
Clark is an important man. It is an honor for him to ask.
Fur trading is a hard life. Perhaps he would be better off with Clark. But he is too young to leave his mother now.
In a year, if you are still willing, we will bring him to you.
Travelers Rest
Great Falls
Fort Mandan
Three Forks
Fort Pierre
Sacagawea traveled 4,356 miles with the expedition. By the time Lewis and Clark returned to their starting point of St. Louis, they had traveled nearly 8,000 miles.

Chapter 4
A Lasting Legend

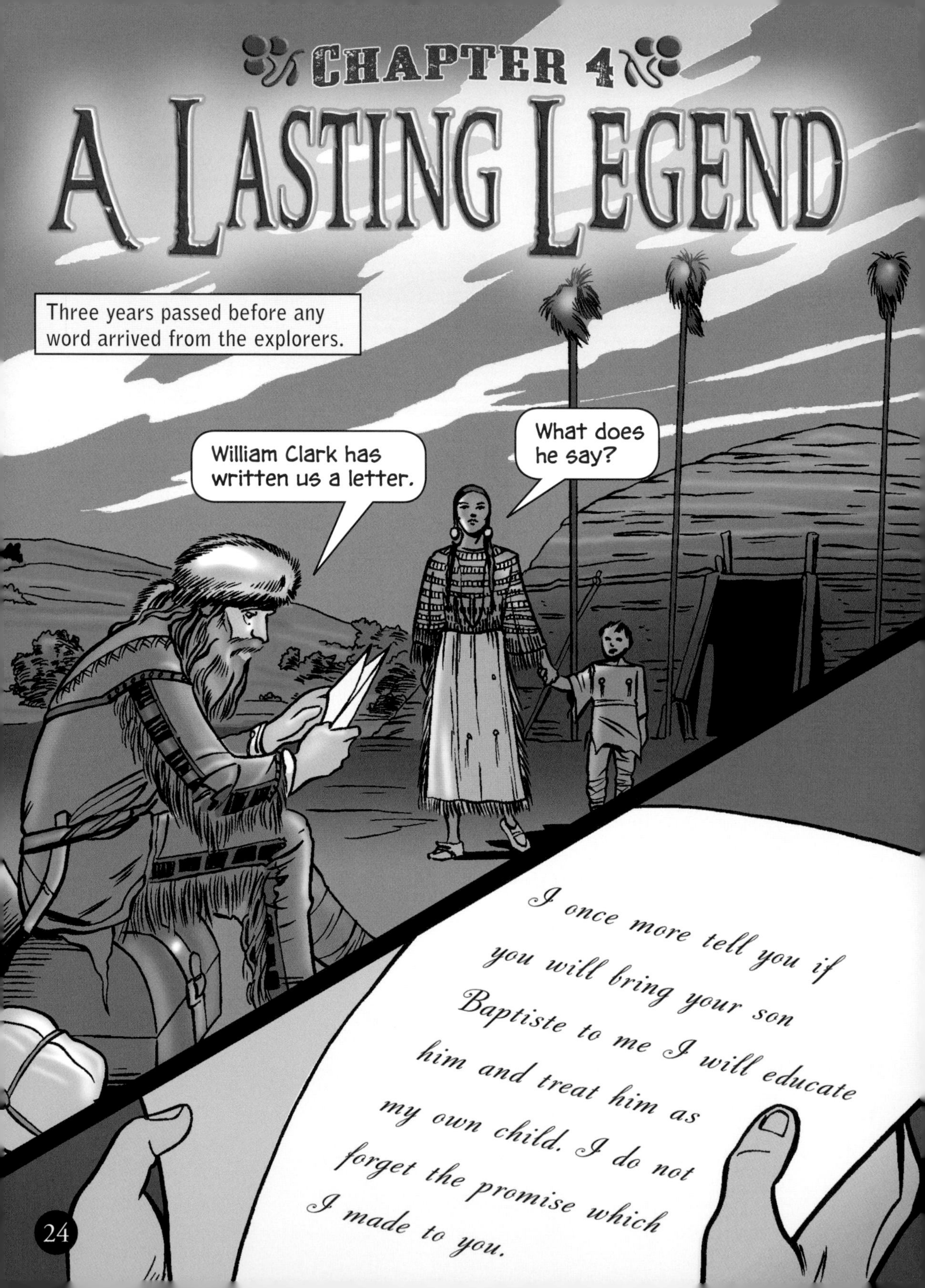

Three years passed before any word arrived from the explorers.
William Clark has written us a letter.
What does he say?
I once more tell you if you will bring your son Baptiste to me I will educate him and treat him as my own child. I do not forget the promise which I made to you.

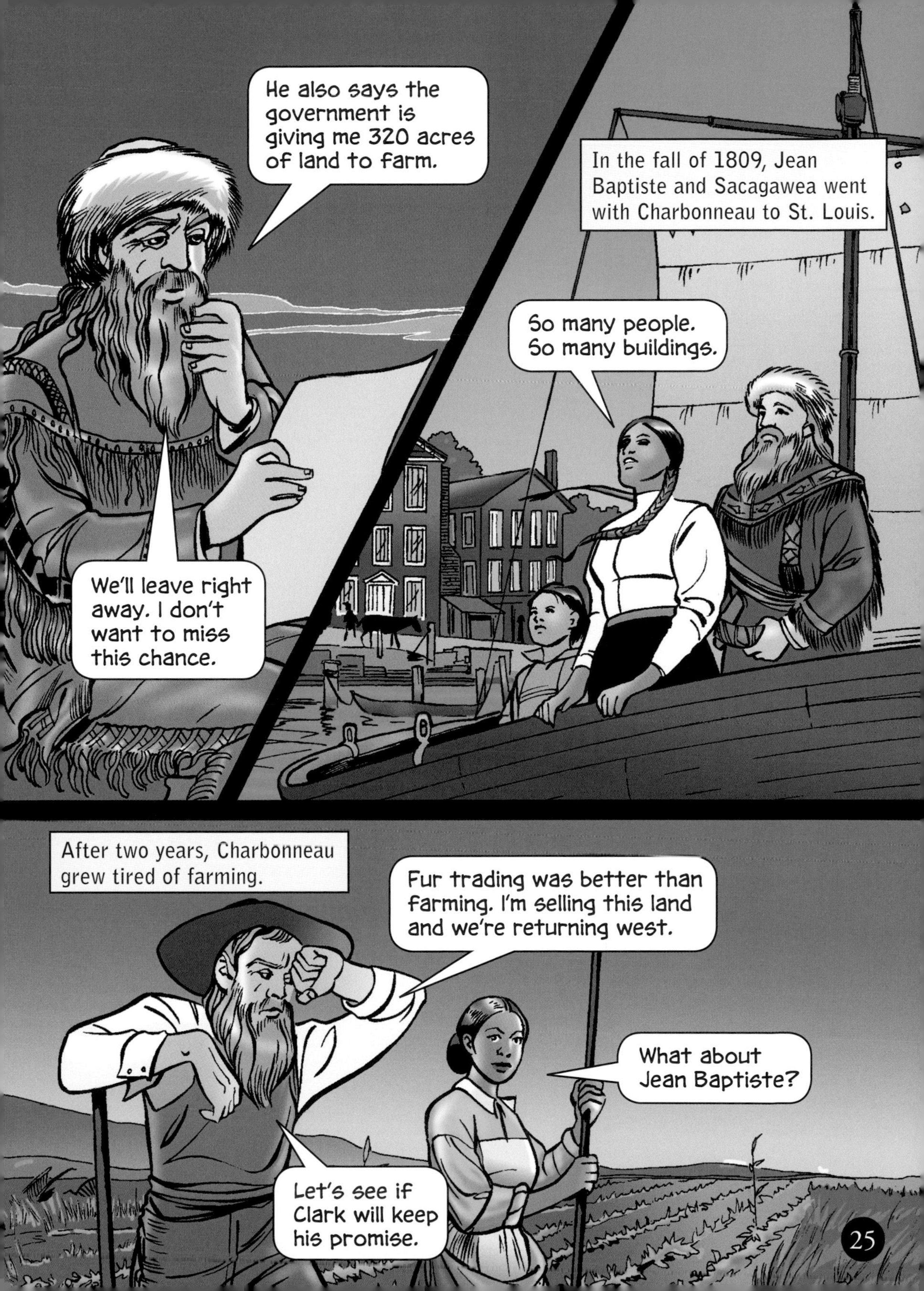
He also says the government is giving me 320 acres of land to farm.
We'll leave right away. I don't want to miss this chance.
In the fall of 1809, Jean Baptiste and Sacagawea went with Charbonneau to St. Louis.
So many people. So many buildings.
After two years, Charbonneau grew tired of farming.
Fur trading was better than farming. I'm selling this land and we're returning west.
What about Jean Baptiste?
Let's see if Clark will keep his promise.

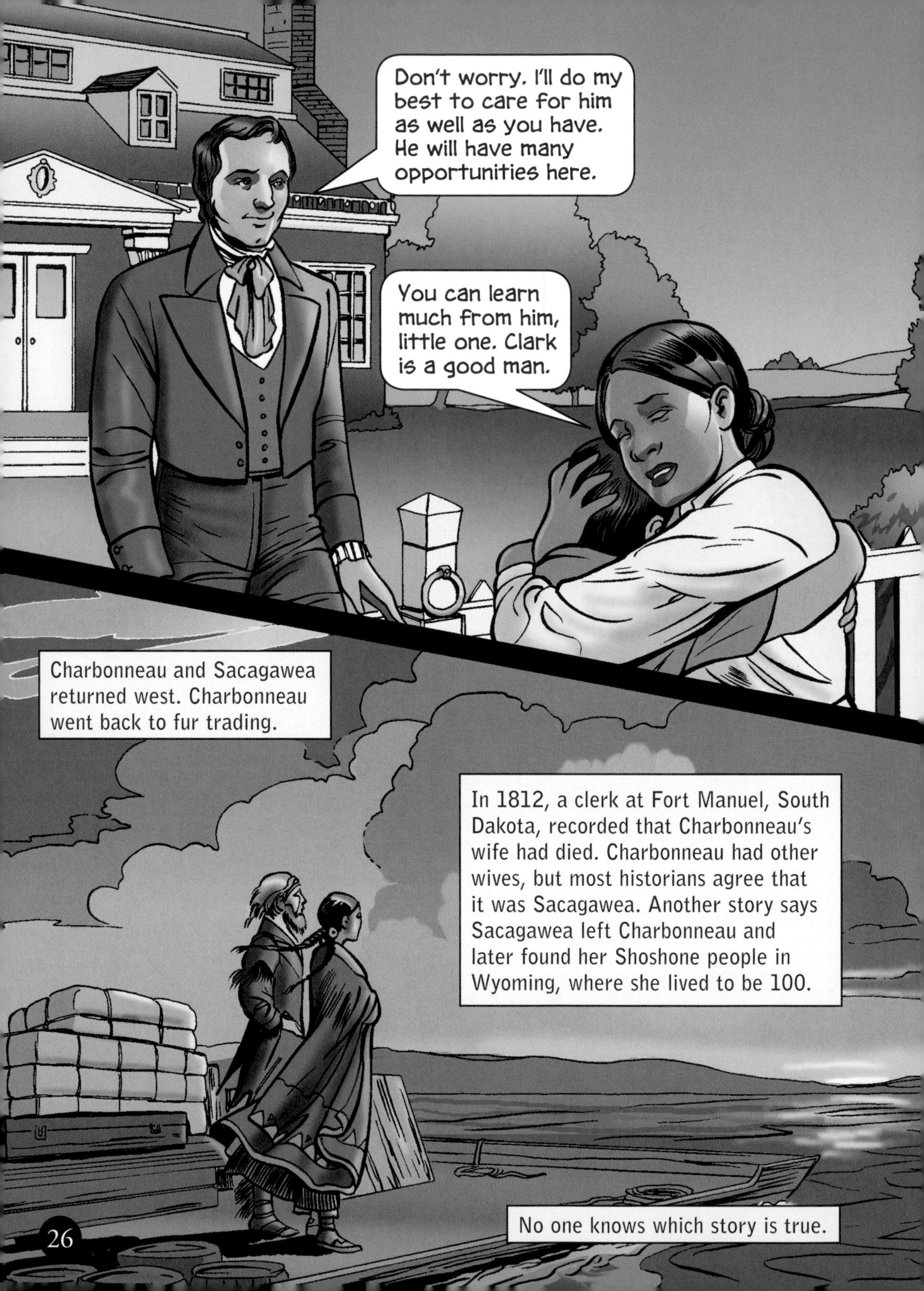
Don't worry. I'll do my best to care for him as well as you have. He will have many opportunities here.
You can learn much from him, little one. Clark is a good man.
Charbonneau and Sacagawea returned west. Charbonneau went back to fur trading.
In 1812, a clerk at Fort Manuel, South Dakota, recorded that Charbonneau's wife had died. Charbonneau had other wives, but most historians agree that it was Sacagawea. Another story says Sacagawea left Charbonneau and later found her Shoshone people in Wyoming, where she lived to be 100.
No one knows which story is true.

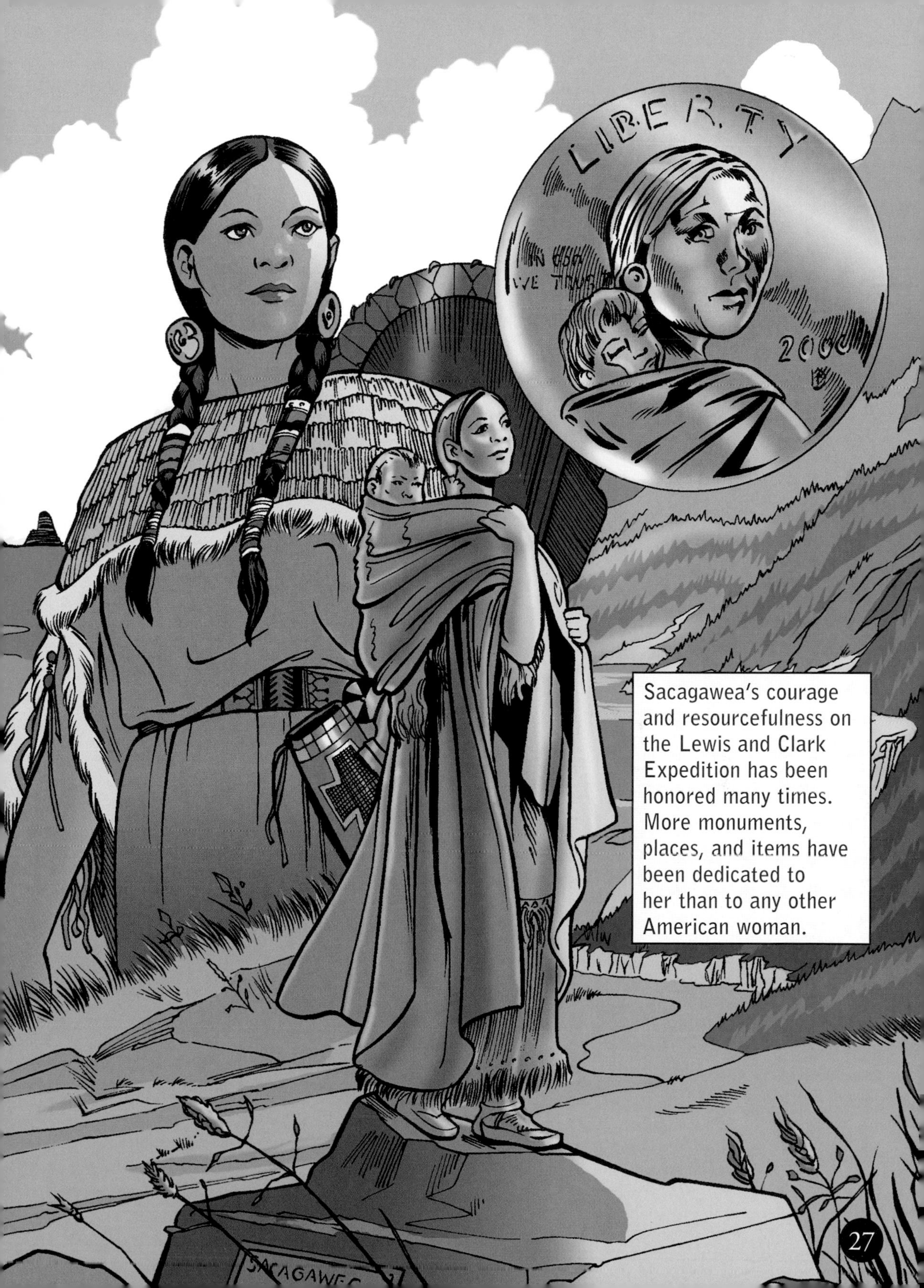
LIBERTY
Sacagawea's courage and resourcefulness on the Lewis and Clark Expedition has been honored many times. More monuments, places, and items have been dedicated to her than to any other American woman.

MORE ABOUT SACAGAWEA

❀ Sacagawea left no written records of her own. Nearly all of what we know about Sacagawea was written in the journals during the Lewis and Clark Expedition.

❀ Sacagawea's name is often mispronounced as "Sacajawea." The Hidatsa did not have a "j" sound in their language. The correct Hidatsa pronunciation is "sa-KAH-ga-wee-ah." *Sacaga* means "bird" and *wea* means "woman." The word "Sacajawea" is a Shoshone word meaning "Boat Launcher."

❀ When the trip was over, Charbonneau was given $500.33 and 320 acres of land for his services as interpreter. Sacagawea received no money. In a letter to Charbonneau, William Clark said Sacagawea deserved more than he had the power to give her.

❀ It is not known if Sacagawea ever saw Jean Baptiste again after she left him with Clark. Jean Baptiste lived in St. Louis until he was 18. He spent six years in Europe before returning to the frontier to become a mountain man.

- Sacagawea may have had another child, a girl named Lisette. The clerk at Fort Manuel recorded that the wife of Charbonneau had left a fine infant girl when she died. Clark adopted both children, but it is not known if Lisette lived past infancy.

- The Lewis and Clark Expedition treated the native tribes they met with respect. One of the goals of the journey was to increase trade between the United States and American Indians. But soon after the expedition, white people began moving west and taking land away from the American Indians. Thousands of American Indians died because of war and disease brought by white people. Some people view the Lewis and Clark Expedition as the beginning of this fateful time in history.

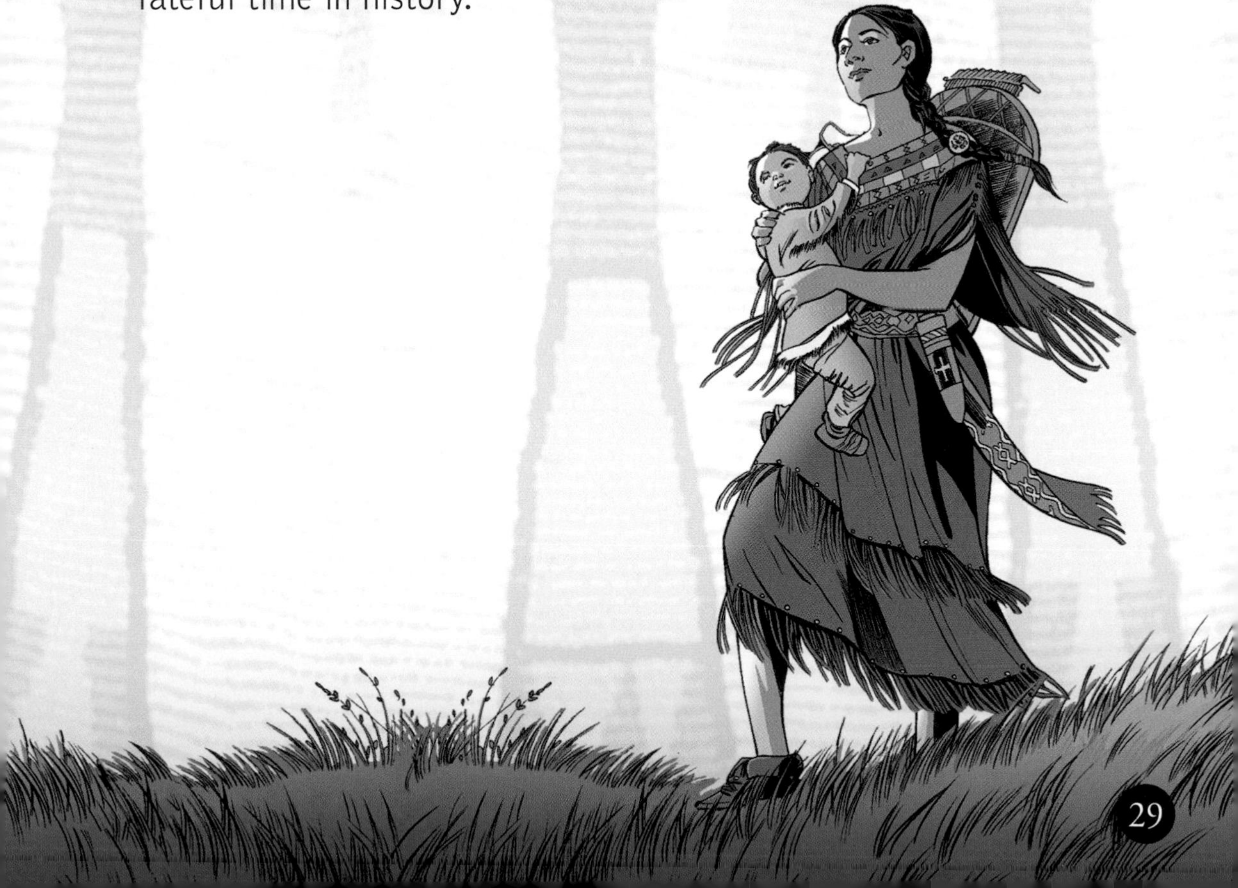

GLOSSARY

camas root (KAM-uhs ROOT)—the edible bulb of the camas lily that grows mainly in the western United States

expedition (ek-spuh-DISH-uhn)—a long trip for a special purpose, such as exploring

pirogue (PEE-rohg)—a canoelike boat

Shoshone (shuh-SHOW-nee)—a group of Native Americans who lived traditionally in present-day Nevada, Idaho, and Utah; Shoshone is also the language of the group.

translate (TRANSS–late)—to write or say something in a different language

tributary (TRIB-yuh-ter-ee)—a stream or river that flows into a larger stream or river

INTERNET SITES

FactHound offers a safe, fun way to find Internet sites related to this book. All of the sites on FactHound have been researched by our staff.

Here's how:
1. Visit *www.facthound.com*
2. Choose your grade level.
3. Type in this book ID **0736864997** for age-appropriate sites. You may also browse subjects by clicking on letters, or by clicking on pictures and words.
4. Click on the **Fetch It** button.

FactHound will fetch the best sites for you!

READ MORE

Gunderson, Jessica. *The Lewis and Clark Expedition.* Graphic Library: Graphic History. Mankato, Minn.: Capstone Press, 2007.

Hunsaker, Joyce Badgley. *Sacagawea Speaks: Beyond the Shining Mountains with Lewis and Clark.* Guilford, Conn.: Two Dot Books, 2001.

Thomasma, Kenneth. *The Truth about Sacajawea.* Jackson, Wyo.: Grandview Publishing, 1997.

BIBLIOGRAPHY

Clark, Ella E., and Margot Edmonds. *Sacagawea of the Lewis and Clark Expedition.* Berkeley, Cal.: University of California Press, 1979.

DeVoto, Bernard, ed. *The Journals of Lewis and Clark.* New York: Houghton Mifflin, 1953.

Hebard, Grace R. *Sacajawea.* Glendale, Cal.: Arthur H. Clark Company, 1957.

Moulton, Gary E., ed. *The Lewis and Clark Journals: An American Epic of Discovery: The Abridgement of the Definitive Nebraska Edition.* Lincoln, Neb.: University of Nebraska Press, 2003.

INDEX